OFFICE SIGNS

essential sign language for the deskbound drone

OFFICE SIGNS

essential sign language for the deskbound drone

Michael Powell

LP

The Lyons Press
Guilford, Connecticut
An imprint of The Globe Pequot Press

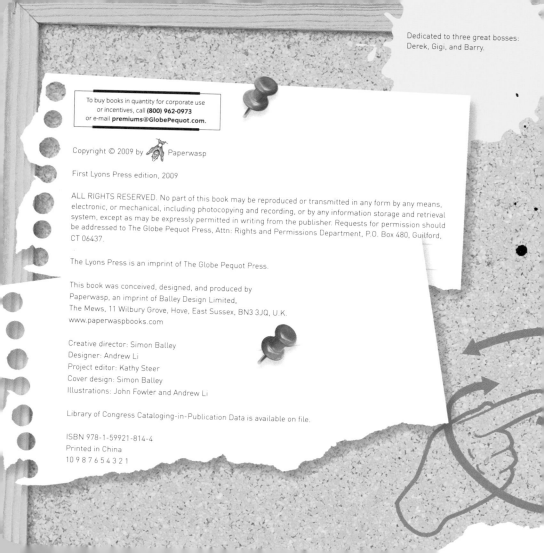

Dedicated to three great bosses:
Derek, Gigi, and Barry.

Copyright © 2009 by Paperwasp

First Lyons Press edition, 2009

The Lyons Press is an imprint of The Globe Pequot Press.

This book was conceived, designed, and produced by
Paperwasp, an imprint of Balley Design Limited,
The Mews, 11 Wilbury Grove, Hove, East Sussex, BN3 3JQ, U.K.
www.paperwaspbooks.com

Creative director: Simon Balley
Designer: Andrew Li
Project editor: Kathy Steer
Cover design: Simon Balley
Illustrations: John Fowler and Andrew Li

Library of Congress Cataloging-in-Publication Data is available on file.

ISBN 978-1-59921-814-4
Printed in China
10 9 8 7 6 5 4 3 2 1

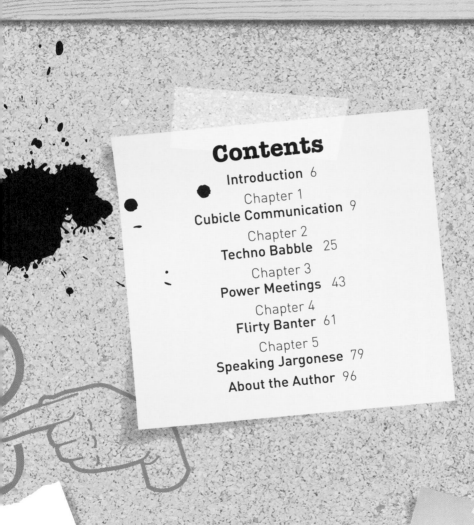

Contents

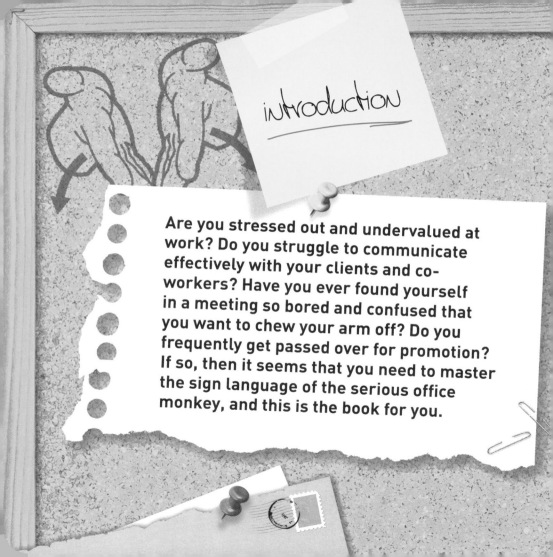

introduction

Are you stressed out and undervalued at work? Do you struggle to communicate effectively with your clients and co-workers? Have you ever found yourself in a meeting so bored and confused that you want to chew your arm off? Do you frequently get passed over for promotion? If so, then it seems that you need to master the sign language of the serious office monkey, and this is the book for you.

Office Signs offers a unique hands-on system of streamlined communications that helps you to interact quickly and clearly with colleagues and clients the world over. It will ensure that you get your point across: gossip when you are lazy, bluff when you are clueless, gripe when you are frazzled, and never again have a dull moment.

Communicate effectively with your friends to achieve what every deskbound drone seeks—that elusive synergy between the simulation of indentured toil and the minimization of actual productive work.

In addition, with a flick of the hand and the flip of a page you'll surely win over whomever you may have your eye on. Ladies, particularly pay attention to the office signs on the left-hand pages and gentlemen, pay attention to those on the right. (However, familiarizing yourself with all of the signs will help you one-up any office tramp or Lothario.)

We're fully aware that manual dexterity is reduced when you've had 17 espressos and a box of donuts, so a yellow sticky note is provided alongside each sign to help you make a judgment call about your digital competence. There's also a response indicator that specifies how quickly you can expect your desired results. Lastly, indulge in our filing cabinet full of "Office Wisdom" that will amuse and demotivate even the most diligent worker. With **Office Signs** at your side, you're onto a winner every time!

Go for it !

Chapter

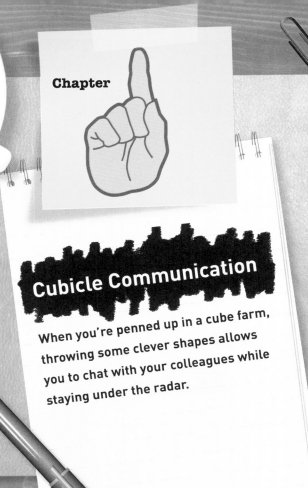

Cubicle Communication

When you're penned up in a cube farm, throwing some clever shapes allows you to chat with your colleagues while staying under the radar.

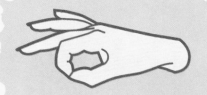

What's up, coworker?

response indicator
(seconds)

easy
medium
hard

Office Wisdom
Don't arrive at work first;
there are no witnesses.

Typical for a Monday.

response indicator (seconds)

easy
medium
hard

Office Wisdom
A company is like a septic tank; the really big chunks rise to the top.

Are you busy?

response indicator
(seconds)

easy
medium
hard

Office Wisdom
Blessed the man who has
found his work—and another
man to do it.

You look stressed. Can I help?

response indicator (seconds)

easy
medium
hard

Office Wisdom
If at first you don't succeed, lock yourself in the restroom and cry until lunch.

I'm having a major crisis.

response indicator
(seconds)

easy
medium
hard

Office Wisdom
If you can't do it well, learn
to enjoy doing it badly.

I'm really unmotivated today.

response indicator (seconds)

easy
medium
hard

Office Wisdom
Hard work never killed anybody, but why take a chance?

You there, fetch me a coffee!

response indicator
(seconds)

easy
medium
hard

Office Wisdom
If you want to get away from the rat race, invest in a sewer.

What have you got for lunch?

response indicator (seconds)

easy
~~medium~~
hard

Office Wisdom
Don't work for peanuts, especially the chocolate coated ones.

I'm on a diet.

response indicator (seconds)

easy
medium
hard

Office Wisdom
Work until your hands bleed—then sue your boss.

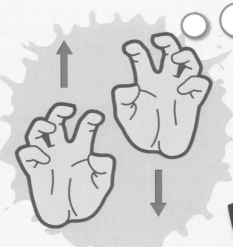

I'm climbing the walls.

response
indicator
(seconds)

easy
medium
hard

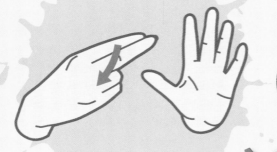

Meet you outside for a smoke in five?

response indicator
(seconds)

easy
medium
hard

Office Wisdom
It takes 20 years of dedicated commitment to become a corporate drone.

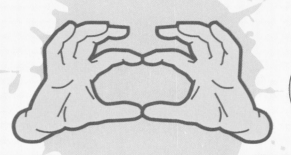

Quick! The donuts have arrived.

response indicator (seconds)

easy
medium
hard

Office Wisdom
Hard work is the cure for everything—except repetitive strain injury.

Is it time to go home yet?

response indicator (seconds)

easy

medium

hard

Office Wisdom
If it wasn't for the last minute, nothing would get done.

I'm leaving early today.

response indicator
(seconds)

easy

medium

hard

Office Wisdom
All work and no play makes Jack a dull boy, and Jill a wealthy widow.

Look busy, the boss is coming.

response indicator (seconds)

easy
medium
hard

Techno Babble

Technology is a double-edged sword with a maddening propensity to prick your dotcom bubble, stab you in the backup, and forward slash your productivity.

My phone won't stop ringing.

response indicator (seconds)

easy
medium
hard

Office Wisdom
"The way to reach the top is to kiss bottom."

I'm on hold.

response indicator (seconds)

easy
medium
hard

Office Wisdom
Try, try, until you succeed,
or at least until the
donuts arrive.

Take a message, I'll call them later.

response
indicator
(seconds)

easy
medium
hard

Office Wisdom
Don't be irreplaceable; if you can't be replaced, you can't be promoted.

Tell them I've left already.

response
indicator
(seconds)

easy
medium
hard

> **Office Wisdom**
> Never do today that which
> will become someone else's
> responsibility tomorrow.

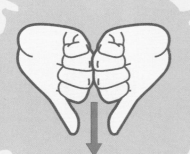

My computer just crashed, again.

response indicator (seconds)

easy
medium
hard

Office Wisdom
Some days you're the photocopier, other days you're the butt cheeks.

I'm multislacking.

response indicator (seconds)

easy
medium
hard

Office Wisdom
If you don't know what you're doing, delegate.

I'm updating my Facebook status.

60

45 15

30

response indicator
(seconds)

easy
medium
hard

Office Wisdom
Indecision is the key to flexibility.

I'm writing my blog.

response indicator
(seconds)

easy

medium

hard

> **Office Wisdom**
> The sooner you fall behind,
> the more time you will have
> to catch up.

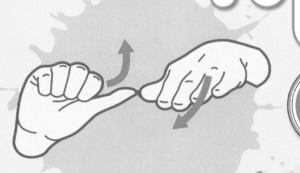

I'm ego-surfing.

response indicator (seconds)

easy
medium
hard

Office Wisdom
To err is human, to forgive is Not Company Policy.

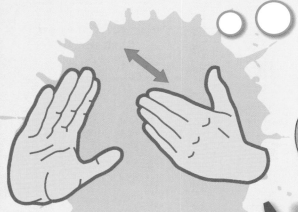

I'm surfing inappropriately.

response indicator (seconds)

easy
medium
hard

Office Wisdom
A fool and his stapler are soon parted.

I've discovered a new flash site.

response indicator
(seconds)

easy
medium
hard

Office Wisdom
Don't think outside the box;
get hired to build a
bigger box.

I'm playing Space Invaders.

response indicator (seconds)

easy
medium
hard

Office Wisdom
It is better to know all of the excuses than some of the answers.

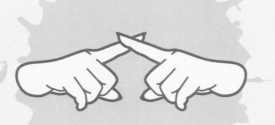

Hey, quit googling me!

response
indicator
(seconds)

easy
medium
hard

Office Wisdom
A fool curses the darkness;
a wise man consults health
and safety procedures.

Get me—I'm actually working!

response indicator (seconds)

60 · 45 · 15 · 30

easy
medium
hard

Office Wisdom
Motivation is what gets you started. Coffee is what keeps you going.

The photocopier is busted.

60

45 **15**

response indicator (seconds)

30

easy

medium

hard

Office Wisdom
No deadline can stand the assault of sustained prevarication.

The coffee machine is kaput.

response
indicator
(seconds)

easy
medium
hard

Office Wisdom
Keep shooting for the moon.
Even if you miss, you'll still
look busy.

I bet the elevator is still out of order.

response indicator (seconds)

easy
medium
hard

Office Wisdom
Ham and eggs—a day's work for a chicken; a lifetime commitment for a pig.

Chapter

Power Meetings

Meetings are the practical alternative to work and where prehensile micromanagement is the counterbalance to being woefully unprepared.

I'm totally making these figures up.

response indicator (seconds)

60
45   15
30

easy
medium
hard

Office Wisdom
After all is said and done, a lot more will be said than done.

Let's resist going into solution mode just yet.

response indicator (seconds)

easy
medium
hard

Office Wisdom
If there is light at the end of the tunnel, order more tunnel.

He's talking out of his butt.

response indicator (seconds)

easy
medium
hard

Office Wisdom
If you're not the lead dog you'll always be looking up someone's ass.

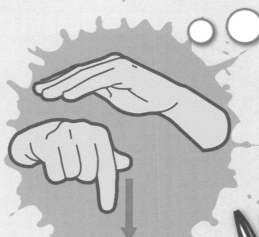

She's out of her element.

response
indicator
(seconds)

easy
medium
hard

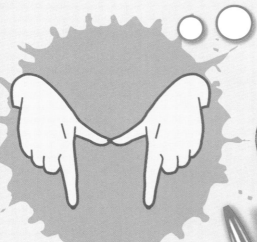

That's non-negotiable.

response indicator (seconds)

60 15 30 45

easy
medium
hard

Office Wisdom
Because most employees are whining idiots, you're probably one of them.

By how much can we overcharge?

response indicator (seconds)

easy
medium
hard

Office Wisdom
Next year, you'll look back on today and start crying all over again.

I need to run this past my immediate superiors.

response indicator (seconds)

easy
medium
hard

Office Wisdom
"If you work for the fun of it, someone else is probably exploiting you."

I'll check on that and get back to you.

response indicator (seconds)

easy
medium
hard

Office Wisdom
A cluttered desk is a sign of empty drawers.

I think we can agree to disagree.

response indicator (seconds)

easy
medium
hard

Office Wisdom
Kissing the same ass doesn't make you a team.

I have one caveat.

response indicator
(seconds)

easy
medium
hard

Office Wisdom
When you're out of your element, lie on your back and go with the flow.

How do we monetize this?

response indicator (seconds)

60
45   15
30

easy
medium
hard

Office Wisdom
Don't limit yourself. You can go as far as the glass ceiling allows.

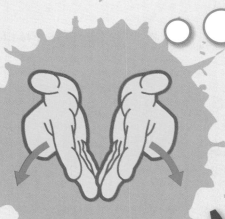

We need a scapegoat.

response
indicator
(seconds)

easy

medium

hard

Office Wisdom
It's always better to kiss butt
than your job goodbye.

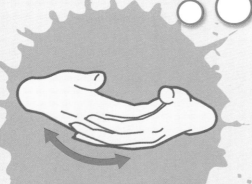

This is your fault.

60
45   **15**
30

response
indicator
(seconds)

easy
medium
hard

Office Wisdom
It's not your salary that
makes you rich, it's what you
take in kickbacks.

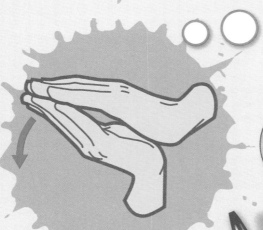

I'm falling asleep here.

response indicator (seconds)

easy
medium
hard

Office Wisdom
Shredding will never catch up with the demand for paperwork.

You're asking too much.

response indicator (seconds)

easy
medium
hard

Office Wisdom
Leap and the net will appear;
or an ambulance.

Our clients look hungry.

response indicator (seconds)

easy
medium
hard

Office Wisdom
An obstacle is often a stepping stone to an insurmountable obstruction.

I need to use the restroom.

60

45   15

30

response indicator (seconds)

easy

medium

hard

Office Wisdom
Monday is an awful way to spend one-seventh of your life.

Chapter

Flirty Banter

What better moment to ramp up the innuendo than when you're being paid for it, because if you get rejected at least it's on someone else's time.

I'd really like to train with you.

response indicator (seconds)

60
45 15
30

easy
medium
hard

Office Wisdom
Mistakes are a fact of life; it is how you pin them on others that counts.

How about a little
horizontal integration?

response
indicator
(seconds)

easy
medium
hard

Office Wisdom
Don't think "obstacle," think
"opportunity to screw
up again."

Can I loop you in?

response
indicator
(seconds)

easy
medium
hard

Office Wisdom
In the land of the blind, the
Seeing Eye dog is king.

I'm the market leader in organic growth.

response indicator
(seconds)

60

45   15

30

easy

medium

hard

Office Wisdom
The best thing about work is that it stops when you're dead.

Let's schedule a fluid transfer.

response indicator
(seconds)

easy
medium
hard

Office Wisdom
It's not the cards you are dealt, it's the gun hidden in your sock.

Let's go open kimono.

response indicator (seconds)

60 · 45 · 15 · 30

easy
medium
hard

Office Wisdom
Cheer up! Things are getting worse at a slower rate.

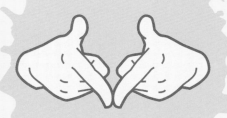

We should definitely touch base.

response indicator (seconds)

easy
medium
hard

Office Wisdom
Cemeteries are full of indispensable people.

I'd like to push your envelope.

response indicator (seconds)

easy
medium
hard

Office Wisdom
There is no right or wrong.
Only statutory procedures.

I've scheduled your meeting in the office supply closet.

response indicator
(seconds)

60

45   15

30

easy
medium
hard

Office Wisdom
We work to retire, not
to acquire.

Bear with me. I'm just performing a cost-benefit analysis.

response indicator (seconds)

60
45
15
30

easy
medium
hard

Office Wisdom
A journey of a thousand miles begins with a single flight reservation.

I'd like us to focus on inbound logistics.

response indicator (seconds)

easy
medium
hard

Office Wisdom
A meeting is an event where minutes are taken and hours are wasted.

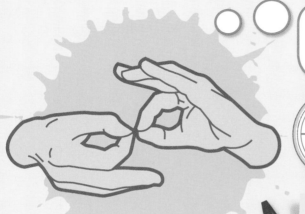

I'd pass through your
value chain any day.

response
indicator
(seconds)

easy
medium
hard

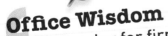

Office Wisdom
Today is the day for firm
decisions! Or is it?

We should dovetail nicely.

response indicator (seconds)

easy
medium
hard

Office Wisdom
Fools rush in where fools have been before.

You auto configure, I'll watch.

response indicator (seconds)

easy
medium
hard

Office Wisdom
When in charge, ponder.
When in trouble, delegate.
When in doubt, mumble.

You've just found yourself a stakeholder.

response indicator (seconds)

easy

medium

hard

Office Wisdom
By doing just a little every day, the task can overwhelm you gradually.

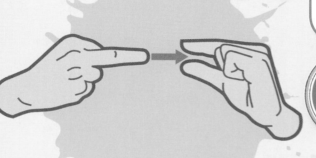

Can I send a data packet to your IP?

response indicator (seconds)

easy
medium
hard

Office Wisdom
It isn't those you fire who make your life miserable, it's those you don't.

How do you feel about a church wedding?

response indicator
(seconds)

60
45
15
30

easy
medium
hard

Office Wisdom
Nepotism may get you to the top, but it takes arrogance to keep you there.

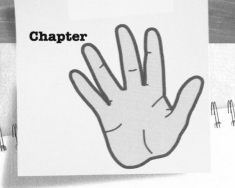

Chapter

Speaking Jargonese

Bring added value to the table and hit the ground running by rolling out impactful signage that delivers 110 percent user satisfaction.

It's a win/win.

response indicator
(seconds)

easy
medium
hard

Office Wisdom
If you want to gather honey,
don't pour coffee on
the beehive.

I'm cautiously optimistic.

response
indicator
(seconds)

easy
medium
hard

Office Wisdom
There is no elevator to the top. You have to climb the walls.

We need to think out of the box.

response indicator (seconds)

Office Wisdom
"Always make tomorrow the busiest day of the week."

easy
medium
hard

We've got to raise the bar.

response indicator (seconds)

easy
medium
hard

Run it up the flagpole.

response indicator (seconds)

easy
medium
hard

Office Wisdom
If God meant us to enjoy work we'd all be Jessica Alba's sponge.

Let's get our ducks in a row.

response indicator
(seconds)

easy
medium
hard

Office Wisdom
There are no menial jobs,
only menial people.

Pick the low-hanging fruit.

response indicator (seconds)

easy
medium
hard

Office Wisdom
Your greatest resource is your time; and your stash of cookies.

Let's get granular.

response indicator
(seconds)

60
45   15
30

easy
medium
hard

Office Wisdom
Retirement kills more people than hard work ever did.

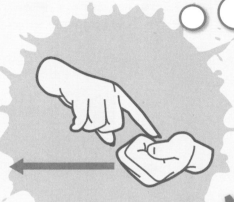

Who moved my cheese?

response indicator
(seconds)

60 45 15 30

easy
medium
hard

Office Wisdom
You don't have to be crazy to work here, but you are.

It's a cash cow.

response indicator (seconds)

easy
medium
hard

Office Wisdom
Teamwork means never having to take all the blame yourself.

It's carbon neutral.

response
indicator
(seconds)

easy
medium
hard

Office Wisdom
According to my calculations,
the problem doesn't exist.

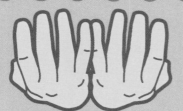

We'd better not let the grass grow too long on this one.

response indicator [seconds]

easy
medium
hard

Office Wisdom
As long as the answer is right, who cares if the question is wrong?

Let's take a thought shower.

response indicator (seconds)

60
45
30
15

easy
medium
hard

Office Wisdom
Tell the boss you were late because your car broke down, next morning it will.

What does M stand for? Empowerment!

response indicator (seconds)

easy
medium
hard

Office Wisdom
Wasting time is an important part of working.

We need to increase our leverage.

response indicator (seconds)

easy

medium

hard

Office Wisdom
Dare to be average.

File for bankruptcy.

response
indicator
(seconds)

easy
medium
hard

Office Wisdom
Lots of people confuse bad
management with destiny.

about the author

MICHAEL POWELL's two greatest passions are idling and using his exquisitely expressive hands for the common good, so he's ideally suited to have written this book. An accomplished humor author with more than 65 titles under his belt including Bar Signs, The Afterlife Handbook, Body Tricks, 101 People You Won't Meet in Heaven, Behave Yourself, and Express Yourself, he lives in a village in Somerset, England with his wife, two children, and a pedigree golden retriever called Feargal Sharkey.